Limits to Relative Performance Evaluation:
Evidence from Bank Executive Turnover

Irina Barakova

Ajay Palvia

Office of the Comptroller of the Currency

OCC Economics Working Paper 2008-3

Version Date: March 10, 2010

Keywords: relative performance evaluation, bank management turnover, governance.
JEL Classifications: G30, G28.

The views expressed in this paper are those of the authors alone and do not necessarily reflect the views of the Office of the Comptroller of the Currency or the U.S. Department of the Treasury. Please address correspondence to the authors at Office of the Comptroller of the Currency, 250 E St. SW, Washington, DC 20219. The authors also can be reached via e-mail at irina.barakova@occ.treas.gov and ajay.palvia@occ.treas.gov.

The authors would like to thank 2009 Eastern Finance Association conference participants, Office of the Comptroller of the Currency seminar participants, Harini Parthasarathy, and David Cicero, for many helpful comments. The authors take responsibility for any errors.

**Limits to Relative Performance Evaluation:
Evidence from Bank Executive Turnover**

**Irina Barakova
Ajay Palvia**

March 2010

Abstract: This paper revisits the topic of relative performance evaluation (RPE) of top management using a large panel of community banks. We show that penalizing executives for poor performance arising from economic downturns is not necessarily inconsistent with the theory. Our empirical results indicate that weak downturn-linked performance is strongly related to increased executive turnover. Furthermore, this relationship is more pronounced in better-governed banks, which are more likely to engage in value-enhancing disciplinary actions. Our analysis suggests that executive dismissals during adverse economic conditions are not necessarily a result of bad luck; rather, the analysis implies that bad times are informative about management quality.

I. Introduction

Although company boards of directors generally cannot directly observe the ability or effort of top management, forcing out badly performing top management is one of their most important responsibilities. Therefore, boards must be able to accurately evaluate top management performance. The most common measure of management performance—firm profitability—may not be adequate, because firm profits are determined in part by factors beyond management's control.[1] Intuitively, an accurate assessment of management performance hinges on accounting for the impact of exogenous factors.

While the exogenous factors affecting a firm's performance are not directly observable, the simultaneous performance of peer firms provides a measure of these factors, because such factors are likely to affect the performance of similar firms at the same time. Holmstrom (1979, 1982) formalizes this reasoning and presents a model showing that common uncertainty can be informative of management's actions; this model provides a theoretical foundation for the evaluation of relative performance. Gibbons and Murphy (1990) further show that if management's actions are independent of exogenous factors, an optimal management compensation package should fully filter out factors outside management's control. Relative performance evaluation (RPE) as defined by Gibbons and Murphy (1990) is intuitive and applicable in many contexts, and has become the standard definition in the literature. However, most empirical studies of RPE find that evaluation of top management is not fully independent of exogenous events.[2] Thus, the applicability of the theoretical result to real-world dismissal

---

[1] We ignore the contribution of all other employees, because top management is accountable for the team's performance.

[2] The RPE empirical literature includes, for example, Aggarwal and Samwick (1999), Bertrand and Mullainathan (2001), Barro and Barro (1990), Garvey and Milbourn (2006), Janakiraman et al. (1992), and Jenter and Kanaan (2008).

decisions for chief executive officers (CEO) is undermined by the evidence (see Jenter and Kanaan 2008). The finding that management discipline is more pronounced during economic downturns is most likely attributable, as suggested by Jenter and Kanaan (2008) either to executives being punished for bad luck or alternatively, firm performance during downturns being a more accurate reflection of management quality.[3] In this paper, we examine these alternative explanations by revisiting the underlying theory and assumptions, and by testing for RPE in a unique dataset of community banks.

First, we consider the suitability of the assumption, made in many empirical RPE studies, that management's actions are independent of the economic environment; we find that if this assumption is relaxed, the theory is not necessarily inconsistent with management being penalized for poor performance linked to exogenous shocks. Next, we test for the presence of RPE using a two-stage approach that separates the exogenously determined portion of performance from its idiosyncratic component and then examines the impact of these separate components on management turnover. We find evidence that bank executive turnover does depend on the exogenous environment, which is inconsistent with strict adherence to RPE. In fact, when the industry sector is experiencing a downturn, only a relatively large improvement in firm performance protects against the probability of management turnover. Further, we show that better-governed banks, whose disciplinary actions are more likely to be well thought-out and value-enhancing, are more likely than poorly governed banks to punish management when exogenously driven performance is weak. Taken together, our results are consistent with the

---

[3] Similarly, Bertrand and Mullainathan (2001) suggest that management is rewarded for good luck.

view that managers are not necessarily punished for bad luck but rather that bad times reveal the quality of management.[4]

We base our empirical study on a large sample of community banks for three reasons. First, past studies that found evidence not fully consistent with RPE have attributed such findings to market pressure. Market pressure may bias the results against finding RPE because negative media and analyst coverage, especially during economic downturns, may lead to top management taking the blame for losses.[5] For example, it has been observed that market forces could affect the payoff (turnover and compensation) of top management, preventing the use of RPE (Fisman, Khurana, and Rhodes-Kropf 2005).[6] Our focus on community banks, which are predominantly private, largely mitigates the possibility of market pressure driving the results.

A second benefit of our dataset is the relatively high level of homogeneity within peer groups. Most of the previous studies of RPE used cross-industry data that treated each industry as a peer group. This may lead to significant heterogeneity within peer groups and introduce significant measurement error, calling the rejection of RPE results into question (Parrino, 1997). The generally homogenous nature of our sample, the explicit account of exogenous factors affecting bank profitability, and our definition of asset-size-based peer groups help minimize this problem.

Finally, to the extent that firms do account for the industry cycle effect on their performance, RPE is more likely to be identified in a cyclical industry such as banking. Because

---

[4] Several possible elements of quality could be better identified during bad times. One key quality, for example, is the ability to aptly manage risk. While managing the risk of financial distress is an important quality for all types of firms, it may be particularly important for bank management. The probability of failure during economic downturns is significant for community banks, and both the owners of the bank and the regulatory agencies could experience losses if the bank goes under because of financial distress.

[5] Top managers are compensated significantly for bearing that risk by generous severance packages.

[6] Consistent with the market pressure story is the hypothesis put forth by Jenter and Kanaan (2008) that management is punished for bad luck.

RPE is applicable only when common uncertainty affects all agents at the same time, not all industries may provide an appropriate context for testing the hypothesis. While there are a few other empirical investigations of RPE for senior management at banks, those studies focus on very small samples of public banks (Barro and Barro 1990) or examine RPE within a firm (Blackwell, Brickley, and Weisbach 1994). Our paper, which uses a broad-based sample of banks over a long time span, makes it easier to explore bank management turnover over a range of economic conditions.[7]

This paper makes several contributions to the literature. On the theoretical front, we show that if the assumption of independence between management actions and exogenous factors made by Gibbons and Murphy (1990) and others is relaxed, principal-agent contracts may not be based exclusively on RPE. Second, our paper is the first, to our knowledge, to explore the issue of RPE in small or predominantly private firms. Our finding—that poor performance attributable to exogenous factors is strongly associated with top management dismissals in our sample of community banks—suggests that disciplining management for exogenously linked performance is not limited to large, publicly traded organizations that may overreact under market pressure or the result of measurement errors that may have plagued earlier studies. Finally, we find evidence that RPE is less likely to occur at better-governed banks, which implies that less reliance on RPE is not driven by poor governance. Because better-governed firms are more likely to make disciplinary decisions that enhance value, we believe that disciplinary actions associated with bad economic times should not necessarily be attributed to bad luck; such actions could be simply because bad times allow for better identification of management quality.

---

[7] Significant cyclical variation existed in the U.S. banking industry during our sample period. The first years of the sample (1985–1987) were characterized by a deteriorating financial condition for banks and a significant number of bank failures; the next few years witnessed even more bank failures, with the peak of the banking crisis around 1989 or 1990. The last three years (1992–1994) witnessed far fewer failures and much better performance industry-wide.

In the next section, we revisit the theory and evidence regarding RPE in the literature. The third section outlines our empirical research design. The fourth and fifth sections describe the data and results. The last section presents our conclusions.

II. Theory and Evidence

The theoretical foundation of RPE is laid out in Holmstrom (1982, 1979) in a principal-agent setting with asymmetric information. The agent takes actions that affect her output but are not observable by the principal. For the agent's incentives to align with the principal's objectives, the agent's payoff must be a function of her actual output.[8] However, if, in addition, the output of different agents is correlated because of dependence on a common exogenous factor, joint performance reflects this factor. With a large number of agents, the average performance is an estimate of the exogenous factor, which helps reveal the actual actions of each agent. In an application of this sufficient statistic result, Holmstrom (1982) shows that in such a setting, a contract based on both individual and average peer performance is superior to a contract based solely on individual performance. The result is obtained when both principal and agent are risk-neutral and also holds for risk-averse agents. This general result is the basis for our empirical tests.

Let firm output y be the stochastic function of the agent's action α and exogenous factor x as shown in equation (1). Note that α could be interpreted in different ways depending on the assumptions, but management actions (or value added) is one of the least restrictive interpretations. As in Holmstrom (1982), we assume that all components of output are normally distributed and, thus, that output is normally distributed. The random disturbance ε is

---

[8] Another way to think about the misalignment of incentives in this principal-agent setting is in terms of horizons. Managers have much shorter horizons than principals, and an optimal action under a short horizon may not be optimal under a longer horizon.

independent of both x and α by definition. Without loss of generality, we can assume that each component has zero mean and output is derived from a linear technology:[9]

$$y_{it} = \alpha_{it} + x_t + \varepsilon_{it} \quad \text{where} \quad \alpha, x, \varepsilon \sim N(\vec{0}, \Sigma) \quad \text{and} \quad \Sigma = \begin{bmatrix} \sigma_x^2 & \sigma_{\alpha x} & 0 \\ \sigma_{\alpha x} & \sigma_\alpha^2 & 0 \\ 0 & 0 & \sigma_\varepsilon^2 \end{bmatrix} \tag{1}$$

The main result from Holmstrom (1982) states that the optimal contract depends on both individual and weighted-average peer output:[10]

$$S_i = f(y_i, \sum_{j=1}^N k_j y_j) \qquad \text{where } k \text{ is the weight of output } y \text{ of firm } j. \tag{2}$$

Under the assumed normality, as in Gibbons and Murphy (1990), we can derive the conditional expectation of the agent's action for a given realization of individual and peer firm output:

$$E(\alpha_{it} \mid y_{1t} ... y_{Nt}) = \frac{\sigma_{\alpha x}}{\sigma_x^2} x_t + \frac{\sigma_x^2 \sigma_\alpha^2 - \sigma_{\alpha x}^2}{\sigma_x^2 \sigma_\alpha^2 + \sigma_x^2 \sigma_\varepsilon^2 - \sigma_{\alpha x}^2} \left(y_{it} - \hat{\beta} \sum_{i=1}^N y_{it} \right)$$

$$\tag{3}$$

$$\text{where} \qquad \hat{\beta} = \frac{2\sigma_{\alpha x} + \sigma_x^2}{\sigma_\alpha^2 + \sigma_\varepsilon^2 + N\sigma_x^2 + 2N\sigma_{\alpha x}}$$

Thus, for testing whether an agent is disciplined solely on the basis of her own actions rather than on exogenous factors, the question of interest is whether the expected action α_{it} is related to

---

[9] Although the coefficients on α and x are set to 1, this is a very general form, as any coefficient on α can be interpreted as part of α, and the loading on the systematic factor can be assumed to be the same for all firms in the peer group. Thus, without loss of generality, the coefficient can be set to 1. In our construction of peer groups, we use characteristics that imply homogeneous exposure to exogenous factors.

[10] This contractual form is shown to also apply to a nonlinear output technology of the form:

$$y_{it} = \alpha_i (x_t + \varepsilon_{it}).$$

the exogenous factor x_t, which is represented by the weighted-average peer performance $\hat{\beta}\sum\limits_{i=1}^{N} y_{it}$.

Given the conditional expectation derived above, the covariance of expected management action/quality and average peer firm performance is non-zero when $\sigma_{ax} \neq 0$:

$$\text{Cov } (E(\alpha_{it}|\ y_{1t}\ ...y_{Nt}), \ \hat{\beta}\sum y_{it}) = N\hat{\beta}\left((\sigma_{ax}^2 + \sigma_x^2\sigma_{ax})/\sigma_x^2\right) \neq 0 \qquad (4)$$

In fact, if σ_{ax} is negative (which, in the context of banking, can be interpreted as managing the risk of financial distress during adverse economic conditions), then the above covariance would be positive for $\sigma_{ax} > -\sigma_x^2$. The covariance of conditionally expected action and the output residual $(y_{it} - \hat{\beta}\sum y_{it})$ (i.e., the idiosyncratic component of output) is also positive, because $\text{Cov}(E(\alpha_i|\ y_{1t}\ ...y_{Nt}), (y_{it} - \hat{\beta}\sum y_{it})) > 0$ by the Cauchy-Schwarz inequality. This implies that management turnover should be negatively correlated with both the weighted-average peer performance and the idiosyncratic residual level of performance.

However, Gibbons and Murphy (1990) assume that the actions α and the exogenous factor x are uncorrelated so that $\sigma_{ax} = 0$. In this way, α_i represents a fixed quality of management, which can be interpreted as ability. This assumption simplifies the conditionally expected agent's α as follows:

$$E(\alpha_i\ |\ y_{1t}...y_{Nt}) = \frac{\sigma_\alpha^2}{\sigma_\alpha^2 + \sigma_\varepsilon^2}\left(y_{it} - \hat{\beta}\sum\limits_{i=1}^{N} y_{it}\right) \qquad where \quad \hat{\beta} = \frac{\sigma_x^2}{\sigma_\alpha^2 + \sigma_\varepsilon^2 + N\sigma_x^2} \qquad (5)$$

In this case, the covariance of expected management quality and average peer firm performance is zero by property of independence of regression residuals and covariates. This is the key result of formulating management RPE as evaluation of management based on complete rather than partial filtering of the impact of exogenous factors from a firm's performance.

Gibbons and Murphy's (1990) RPE test is based on the observation that the conditional expectation of management's ability under RPE is positively related to the individual firm's performance and negatively related to the average peer firm performance. This is the weak form of the hypothesis, because even though the regression results do not reject RPE, they do not imply that there is complete filtering of the exogenous factors from executive evaluation.[11] Janakiraman, Lambert, and Larcker (1992) apply a constraint test to the coefficients from Gibbons and Murphy (1990) using the same executive compensation data and reject RPE.

A narrower interpretation of RPE is tested in Barro and Barro (1990), which imposes that $\beta_i = 1/N$ where N is the number of peer firms. Using 83 public banks during 1982–1987, they reject RPE in most specifications. However, the Holmstrom (1982) result does not imply that the contract must depend only on the difference between the performance of the agent and the average performance of her peers.

Bertrand and Mullainathan (2001) derive the testable implication from the conditional expectation of α_i in equation (5) that Cov $(E(\alpha_i| y_{1t} \ldots y_{Nt}), \hat{\beta} \sum y_{it}) = 0$. In essence, they treat the systematic factor as an instrumental variable for the unobservable ability, which is expected to be correlated both with firm performance and with compensation or turnover. The identifying

---

[11] A linear model of turnover under a correlated peer performance would be as follows:

$$\text{TURNOVER}_{i,t} = \gamma_1 \text{PERF}_{i,t-1} + \gamma_2 \text{PEER\_PERF}_{i,t-1} + \zeta_{i,t} = \gamma_1 (\alpha_{i,t-1} + \beta_1 \text{PEER\_PERF}_{i,t-1}) + \gamma_2 \text{PEER\_PERF}_{i,t-1} + \zeta_{i,t}$$

There is an identification problem because $\gamma_2 = -\gamma_1 \beta_1$, and the failure to reject the weak form of RPE could be driven by the level of correlation β_1.

assumption is that peer average provides no information on a firm's management ability. They find a significant coefficient for this variable in a sample of public firms and reject the strong form RPE in a model of executive compensation, which they interpret as evidence of pay for luck.

Jenter and Kanaan (2008) also use the fact that the expected management value added is positively correlated with the idiosyncratic component of performance shown in equation (5) as the testable implication for the strong form of RPE (i.e., that turnover should not be correlated with average peer firm performance). They also reject RPE in a model of turnover in cross-industry public firms. They entertain several explanations, for which they find inconclusive support. The two most supported competing explanations are that managers are blamed for bad luck and that bad times are more reflective than good times of management's ability. In a way, our study formalizes the latter interpretation by pointing out that, theoretically, management's value added does not need to be independent of the economic environment.

Albuquerque (2009) argues that a lack of strong support for RPE in the literature may be driven in part by incorrectly defined peer groups. Using a large cross-industry sample, Albuquerque shows that when peer groups are defined by both industry and size, relative performance is strongly associated with increased managerial discipline, although she does not find complete filtering of exogenous factors. Albuquerque further argues that while firm size might not be the only metric one can use to identify peers within an industry (because size is likely to be monotonically correlated with many other factors that differentiate firms), it is one of the best metrics available. Finally, because firm size is readily available and peer performance based on size is easily computable, it is a plausible and practical method of evaluating RPE implementation by firms in an industry.

III. Research Design

To test for the presence of RPE, we decompose firm performance in terms of exogenously determined and idiosyncratic components, then evaluate the impact of each component on the likelihood of executive turnover. Following Jenter and Kanaan (2008), we use a two-stage approach. The first stage is a model of firm performance; the second stage is a model of executive turnover.

a) First-Stage Analysis: Decomposition of Performance

In cross-industry studies—in which the explicit exogenous factors might be too numerous to control for directly—average industry performance is the only available performance benchmark (Bertrand and Mullainathan 2001; Jenter and Kanaan 2008). Because our analysis is focused on one industry segment, we can control for both the explicit exogenous factors driving profitability and the peer average performance, which can be interpreted as the implicit factor. Similar to Jenter and Kanaan (2008), we estimate a model of performance as a function of exogenous factors, but we use a multifactor model that allows us to better identify the exogenously determined component of performance. Our first-stage specification is as follows:

$$PERF_{i,t} = \beta_0 + \beta_1 PEER\_PERF_{i,t} + \beta_2 FACTORS_t + \upsilon_{i,t} \qquad (6)$$

Using the estimates from equation (6), we can forecast the exogenously determined component of performance or expected performance given average peer group performance and other exogenous factors discussed in the next section. To the extent various exogenous factors are correlated, the use of multiple factors may lead to biased coefficients. However, any potential bias in individual coefficients does not pose a problem, because the first-stage model is to be used for forecasting only. We define exogenous performance as follows:

$$EX\_PERF_{i,t} = \hat{\beta}_0 + \hat{\beta}_1\ PEER\_PERF_{i,t} + \hat{\beta}_2\ FACTORS_t \qquad (7)$$

The residual, $(PERF_{i,t} - EX\_PERF_{i,t})$, is orthogonal to $EX\_PERF_{i,t}$ by definition and can be interpreted as the idiosyncratic component of performance or top management's value added. For our test of RPE, we evaluate the sensitivity of turnover to both the exogenous and the residual component.

The model employs homogeneous peer groups for estimating equation (6), so the average peer performance $PEER\_PERF_{i,t}$ is a good measure of the implicit exogenous factors for each bank. The size of the firm determines, to a large extent, its vulnerability to external factors (Albuquerque 2009). In a way, a well-defined homogeneous peer group should yield the same coefficients if estimated for each firm individually.[12] In our case, the sample for testing RPE is already relatively homogeneous. Focusing on one industry and a particular sector—community banks—ensures that the banks in the sample are affected by the same or similar exogenous factors. Although these banks are already small, there is some size variation, which could affect a bank's ability to withstand exogenous shocks. Therefore, consistent with Albuquerque (2009), we further segment peer groups by asset quartile.[13]

---

[12] In fact, Jenter and Kanaan (2008) do estimate separate coefficients for each firm's performance regressed on the industry average; they find that the coefficients vary significantly.

[13] We test variations in our peer definitions for robustness and discuss these tests later in the paper.

b) Second-Stage Analysis: Testing for RPE

Bertrand and Mullainathan (2001) test the effect of actual and expected exogenous performance on executive compensation in two separate regressions; they reject RPE on evidence that expected performance has similar coefficients to actual performance. In a logistic regression model of turnover, the coefficient estimates for the exogenously determined performance would be biased if the idiosyncratic component of performance were excluded.[14] Similar to Jenter and Kanaan (2008), we include both the exogenously determined $EX\_PERF_{i,t-1}$ and the idiosyncratic component of performance ($PERF_{i,t-1} - EX\_PERF_{i,t-1}$). Thus, our main specification is the following logistic regression:

$$\ln (TURNOVER_{i,t} / (1 - TURNOVER_{i,t})) =$$
$$= \gamma_0 + \gamma_1 (PERF_{i,t-1} - EX\_PERF_{i,t-1}) + \gamma_2 EX\_PERF_{i,t-1} + \gamma_3 CONTROLS + \zeta_{i,t} \qquad (8)$$

Unlike the weak test of RPE, our test can interpret the coefficients γ_1 and γ_2, because the two components ($PERF_{i,t-1} - EX\_PERF_{i,t-1}$) and $EX\_PERF_{i,t-1}$ are not correlated by construction. The RPE null hypothesis is that exogenously determined performance does not affect likelihood of turnover (i.e., $\gamma_2 = 0$). Our alternative hypothesis is that the impact of the exogenous and idiosyncratic components should be directionally similar (i.e., $\gamma_2 < 0$). While rejecting our null hypothesis would strengthen the evidence that executives pay a price for poor performance in economic downturns, such a finding does not help in identifying whether such disciplinary

---

[14] When this second stage involves a logistic regression, as in a model of binary turnover variable, the use of the forecasted portion of performance $EX\_PERF_{i,t-1}$ alone is not sufficient, because the residual differences between the actual and the exogenously determined performance that represent the idiosyncratic component of performance become an omitted variable. Unlike a linear regression, a logistic regression that omits a variable—even if that variable is uncorrelated with the rest of the covariates—leads to bias in the coefficients. For further discussion, see Yatchew and Griliches (1985) and Jenter and Kanaan (2008).

actions are value-enhancing. To explore this issue further, we also examine the effect of governance on the sensitivity of turnover and exogenously determined performance.

c) Governance and RPE

Effective monitoring mechanisms have often been found to be a factor in executive turnover (Borokhovich, Parrino, and Trapani 1996; Dahya, McConnell, and Travlos 2002; Ertugrul and Krishnan 2008; Fisman et al. 2005; Weisbach 1988) and to be linked to RPE (Bertrand and Mullainathan 2001; DeFond and Park 1999; Garvey and Milbourn 2006; Kaplan and Minton 2006). In particular, several of these studies find that performance-turnover sensitivity is positively related to better governance. Weisbach (1988), for example, finds that the relationship between previous performance and CEO resignation is stronger for firms with more outside directors.

We use previous evidence relating increased managerial discipline and better governance to examine whether poor governance could hamper the use of RPE in our sample of community banks. We test for the effect of governance on RPE by re-estimating equation (8) while interacting the two performance components with firms' governance quality. An implicit assumption in the literature is that good governance is value-enhancing; we expect that if management dismissals for poor exogenously determined performance are value-enhancing, such dismissals should be more prevalent among better-governed firms.[15]

---

[15] Better governance—which is usually interpreted as better alignment of owner-manager incentives—is implicitly assumed to be value-enhancing in most of the corporate finance literature. In fact, Gompers and colleagues (2003) and Bhagat and Bolton (2008) explicitly find that certain measures of strong governance are positively associated with better firm performance.

IV. Data

All U.S. commercial banks with assets of $100 million or less were required to report the turnover of senior management on a quarterly basis between 1985 and 1994. This paper uses these unique turnover data, obtained from publicly available bank statements of income and condition (i.e., call reports), to examine the extent of RPE in community banks.[16] Because of the reporting requirements, our study is limited to the years 1985 to 1994; however, the enormous variation in industry financial condition and the long time span of these data are ideal for examining the effects of exogenous and idiosyncratic factors on performance and executive turnover. During this period, even with the $100 million asset-size restriction, our dataset covers around 75 percent of banks. These are mostly private banks, which allows us to ascertain whether RPE is practiced in the absence of market pressure affecting the large, publicly traded firms.

Like the turnover data, all our financial data come from bank statements of income and condition (call reports). Other data come from multiple sources. Unemployment data are from the Bureau of Labor Statistics and Treasury bill rates from the Federal Reserve. Proprietary regulatory ratings, which we use to create our bank governance measure, are from the Office of the Comptroller of the Currency for all national banks.[17]

The final dataset consists of 86,504 bank-year observations in the first stage (where we do not use the supervisory ratings data) and 18,944 bank-year observations in the second stage. These data form an unbalanced panel, because banks remain in the sample for different lengths

---

[16] Although no formal definition exists for "community banks," these institutions are generally characterized as smaller and geographically concentrated banks. Consistent with our available data, we define community banks as commercial banks with assets of $100 million or less.

[17] National banks, overseen by the Office of the Comptroller of the Currency make up roughly one-fourth of all U.S. commercial banks. While the regulatory-based governance variable does reduce our second-stage sample significantly, it is still a large nationally represented sample and more broad-based than those in most previous studies.

of time during the observation period (as new banks come into being and some existing banks grow, merge, or exit). We did not restrict the sample to banks that remained in the sample over the entire period, because this would have greatly reduced the sample size and would have led to considerable survivorship bias. All financial variables are winsorized (by transforming the extreme values) at the bottom 1 percent and top 1 percent levels to minimize the effect of erroneous data points and outliers.

a) Variables: Estimation of Idiosyncratic and Exogenous Performance

The first-stage regressions, as described in the previous section, decompose idiosyncratic and exogenous performance by peer group. Because our study is focused on private firms, we measure performance using accounting returns rather than stock returns.[18] We use two primary measures of performance: return on assets (ROA) and four-quarter change in return on assets (CH_ROA). We also use annual data to reduce seasonality. In the first stage, we model bank performance as a function of explicit and implicit exogenous factors.

The explicit factors used in the first stage of the analysis are the average three-month Treasury bill rate (TBILL), the state unemployment rate (URATE), and the number of banks per million persons in the state (BANKSPCAP). The inclusion of TBILL and URATE helps control for the effects of economic conditions on profitability. The variable BANKSPCAP should help control for the effect of competition.[19] The primary implicit exogenous factor used in the first stage is the average performance in the peer group (ROA_PEER). As an additional implicit

---

[18] Previous studies of public firms have tested RPE on accounting data with similar results.

[19] The most common measure of competition in banking is the Herfindahl Index (HI), which is not available for the entire period of our analysis. Our measure—the number of banks per capita (by state)—is a convenient substitute. For the years when both measures are available, the correlation between a state-level HI and the number of banks per capital is high (about -0.51).

factor, the first-stage regressions include yearly averages for ROA for the whole sector of community banks (YEAR_ROA). Finally, for each explicit and implicit factor, we include not only the level of the factor but also the year-over-year change in the factor. Panel A in table 1 provides descriptive statistics for the explanatory variables used in the first stage of the analysis.

b) Variables: Estimation of the Effect of Performance Components on Turnover

We measure management turnover using a variable indicating any change in senior executives during the year (EXTURN). Consistent with the available data, a senior executive officer is defined as one of the top three officers in the bank; these officers, regardless of their official titles, perform the functions of CEO, president, or senior lending officer. A limitation of these data is that we are not able to exclude voluntary resignations, retirement, or death as reasons for change in top management. Kaplan and Minton (2006) argue that "voluntary" turnover is probably rarely voluntary based on their finding that forced and unforced management turnover exhibit similar patterns.[20] Jenter and Kanaan (2008) find that for voluntary turnover there is no effect of the exogenously determined performance; thus, the existence of significant voluntary turnover in the data would strengthen the support for RPE. To partially correct for voluntary resignation, we also control for outside similar job opportunities. As for retirement and death, there is no reason to believe these alternative causes of executive turnover will be correlated with performance; thus, the limitation of the indicator variable we use introduces noise rather than bias in the results, which we discuss in the next section.

Because our dataset includes a large panel of predominantly private banks, typical governance data used in earlier studies on public companies are not available. Instead, we use the

---

[20] Often CEOs are pressured to resign but are not directly dismissed and technically such turnovers would not be classified as forced.

proprietary CAMEL (capital, asset quality, management, earnings, and liquidity) regulatory ratings to proxy for bank governance.[21] Several past studies have suggested that weak bank regulatory ratings are indicators of poor bank governance. Cook, Hogan, and Kieschnick (2004), Houston and James (1993), and Prowse (1995), for example, suggest that poor regulatory ratings or other regulatory censures are linked to executive dismissals or turnover. Gunther and Moore (2003) suggest that regulatory rating downgrades are associated with banks not fully disclosing their losses. Finally, Cooper (2008) shows that strong regulatory ratings are associated with better performance and better director pay. Implicitly or explicitly, these studies suggest that regulatory censure or weak regulatory ratings are associated with poor governance.

While many types of regulatory information may implicitly capture information about governance, we focus on the regulatory rating of bank management (MRATING).[22] Regulatory ratings of bank management are defined as a summary measure of regulatory opinion of management competence, leadership, administration ability, planning ability, depth and succession, and self-dealing tendencies. These ratings are particularly well suited to measuring management quality or governance. Regulatory ratings of bank management range from 1 (best) to 5 (worst); ratings of 1 and 2 are generally considered "good," while ratings of 3, 4, or 5 are usually considered "poor."[23]

Several other variables are included in the second stage to control for basic bank attributes. We include the capital ratio, based on Tier 1 capital (CAPRAT), to represent the

---

[21] The supervisory CAMEL ratings are the summary evaluations of bank conditions; they are revisited during on- and offsite supervision. Unlike rating agency ratings, the supervisory ratings are not shared with the public. Each component of CAMEL, as well as the overall composite CAMEL, is rated on a scale of 1 (best) to 5 (worst).

[22] In robustness tests (described later in the paper), we discuss tests that verify MRATING as a suitable indicator of bank governance.

[23] The supervisory rating of management is the M component of supervisory CAMEL ratings.

financial leverage or the level of the institution's safety cushion. We control for size with the log of total assets (LGASSET).

We also include a set of variables to control for organizational factors that may explain turnover. First among these is a dummy indicating whether the bank has acquired another bank during the year (ACQUIRE); banks that have acquired other banks are more likely to have redundant management and, thus, more likely to have higher executive turnover. Additionally, because newer banks are likely to have less-experienced management, the likelihood of management turnover could be different for these banks, which we account for with a dummy indicating that the bank was chartered within the past five years (DENOVO).[24]

Though we cannot obtain ownership structure for our sample of banks, we can identify whether an unaffiliated bank becomes a member of a bank holding company, whether a bank changes its affiliation from one holding company to another, and whether a bank in a holding company becomes unaffiliated. Using this information, we construct a measure of change in ownership (OWNCHANGE) indicating any of the above changes. To the extent that these changes lead to redundant or insufficient management, executive changes may result. We include a dummy indicating affiliation in a multibank holding company (MBHC), because these organizations may have more complicated board and management structures that might affect executive turnover.[25]

To control for the effect of market factors on turnover, we include additional variables. The first is a measure to capture the effect of competition on turnover; as in the first stage, we measure competition using the number of banks per million persons in the state (BANKSPCAP).

---

[24] Given that these banks can differ significantly in many ways, we have also confirmed our results when excluding the DENOVO banks.

[25] As a robustness exercise, we also consider the effect of multibank holding company banks by excluding such banks from the analysis altogether. The results do not change when these banks are excluded.

The next measure is meant to proxy for involuntary turnover. While our data do not allow us to separate voluntary and involuntary turnover directly, we use the fact that executives are more likely to leave voluntarily when outside opportunities exist. Thus, our last control is an indicator of the percentage of *other* banks in the city with turnover (EXTURNCITY). Panel B in table 1 describes the national banks and variables used in the second stage of the analysis.

V. Results and Interpretations

Both bank performance and turnover in community banks are cyclical, as can be seen in panel A of figure 1. This by itself provides some contradiction of RPE, because the assumed independence of management quality and exogenous shocks under the hypothesis implies that the portion of poor quality managers is not expected to be clustered across time. The bottom two panels further show the cyclical nature of the exogenous conditions affecting bank performance during the period. Panel B presents the macroeconomic environment in terms of average state unemployment and interest rates over time. Panel C tracks the average number of banks per capita in the state as a measure of bank competition. The length of the period allows for sufficient dynamics of the exogenous factors to exhibit a relationship with management turnover, and these graphs, taken together, clearly suggest that turnover is not driven entirely by RPE. Our two-stage empirical model tests these observed relationships in a more complete multivariate framework.

a) First-Stage Analysis

Performance varies across banks, because it depends on their ability to absorb shocks. The peer groups described in the previous section are created to provide a proper benchmark for expected bank performance. Panel A in table 2 shows summary statistics for each of the four peer groups, indicating that they are different. We can see from this table that peer performance depends on size, because smaller banks have larger increases in ROA and larger banks have larger absolute values for ROA. Similarly, market conditions (proxied by URATE and BANKSPCAP) suggest that banks of different sizes are affected differently by shocks.

The model in the first stage of our analysis—equation (6)—estimates the loadings on the different exogenous determinants of performance. The fit of the model is relatively good for a regression of change in accounting performance. Numerous individual characteristics could improve the explanatory power of the model, but this is not the purpose of the first stage; rather, we want to include only factors that are beyond management's control, at least in the short term. The coefficients from the first stage are hard to interpret owing to multicollinearity, as the industry and peer performance, unemployment, and interest rates are all significantly correlated.[26] In panel B of table 2, we report univariate correlations with all the exogenous factors in the model for each of the peer groups in order to show the difference in factor loadings across factors and across peer groups. The results suggest that the impact of exogenous factors depends on bank size, confirming that segmenting by size is reasonable.[27] For example, peer performance tends to have a much larger impact for larger banks, from 4 percent to 9 percent. Similarly, performance is more highly correlated with the sector average performance for larger community banks than for small banks, while small banks' performance depends more on changes in the local unemployment rate.[28]

---

[26] Multicollinearity is not an issue in using the model estimates for forecasting, which is our main purpose (i.e., to disentangle the exogenously determined from the idiosyncratic component of performance).

[27] As a robustness test, we also define peer groups in terms of tertiles and quintiles of size.

[28] While the first-stage regressions include yearly averages for the implicit factors as well, we do not report these in table 2 for conciseness and because they do not vary by peer.

The forecasted performance from the first-stage estimates is the expected or exogenously determined performance. The difference between the actual and exogenously determined performance is the idiosyncratic component of performance. The mean exogenously determined performance is 0.76 percent with a standard deviation of 0.32 percent, while—as expected—the mean idiosyncratic performance is almost zero with a standard deviation of 1 percent. By design, the two components are orthogonal, and regressing the management turnover indicator on these measures yields coefficients that show the impact of each component and allows us to directly test the RPE hypothesis.

b) Second-Stage Analysis

The results from the main specification of the turnover model are presented in the first column in table 3. The coefficients on individual and exogenous performance are both negative and significant; thus, we reject the hypothesis that banks evaluate management in purely relative terms. Strengthening the results of Jenter and Kanaan (2008), who provide cross-industry evidence of limited filtering of exogenous performance, we find that for our community bank sample, the effect of the exogenously determined performance change on turnover likelihood is at least as large as and usually larger than the effect of individual performance. The results are reported using ROA as the measure of performance in columns 1–3 and CH_ROA as the measure of performance in columns 4–6.

Previous literature has suggested that the lack of RPE evidence may be owing to top management's entrenchment and poor firm governance. We compare our results of the turnover model with and without controlling for bank governance. Although the relationship between the likelihood of turnover and performance is weaker when we include our governance control, the general RPE result is preserved. The second and fifth columns show that the rejection of RPE is not a result of poor governance. As expected, worse governance (indicated by a higher MRATING) is associated with more turnover. This suggests that worse governance leads to more management dismissals.[29]

To allow for other characteristics for which we do not control, we also estimate our results with peer fixed effects, as did Jenter and Kanaan (2008). The results do not change substantially when peer effects are included (see columns 3 and 6).[30] The results in column 3 indicate that a 1 percent decrease in idiosyncratic performance leads to a 23.4 percent increase in the log odds, while the same change in exogenous performance leads to a 38.6 percent increase in the log odds. Note, however, that while 1 standard deviation for the idiosyncratic component of performance is around 1 percent, the exogenously determined performance varies much less, so a 1 standard deviation change of 0.3 percent leads to only a 12 percent increase in the log odds.

Consistent with the view that management dismissals attributable to poor exogenously linked performance are value-enhancing, we expect the impact of exogenously determined performance on executive turnover to be stronger in better-governed banks. To examine this issue, we re-estimate our turnover regression; but rather than including the performance terms directly, we include these terms interacted with indicators of good or poor governance. As before, we measure governance using MRATING and define good governance as an MRATING of 1 or 2 and poor governance as an MRATING of 3, 4, or 5.

---

[29] While these dismissals can be attributed to some extent to regulatory pressure on poorly governed firms, they are nevertheless the result of poor governance, and this distinction is not vital to our analysis. We return to this issue in the robustness section.

[30] We also estimate these results with bank fixed effects. The results are in the same direction, but the significance is weaker and not all specifications are significant. This indicates that we do not have enough observations for each bank to make meaningful inferences when we include bank fixed effects.

The results of these additional tests are described in table 4. Columns 1–3 show results with ROA as the measure of performance, and columns 4–6 show results with CH_ROA as the measure of performance. Each column in table 4 shows that better-governed banks exhibit a much stronger relationship between exogenously determined performance and turnover. The results are robust to the direct effect of governance (columns 2 and 5) and to the peer fixed effects (columns 3 and 6). The coefficients from column 3 imply that the negative impact of EX_PERF on turnover under good MRATING is 70 percent higher than the impact under poor MRATING. Similarly, IND_PERF affects turnover 60 percent more when management is highly rated than when it is not.

Because both elements of performance exhibit stronger performance-turnover sensitivity in better-governed firms, the results indicate that overall bank performance has higher performance-turnover sensitivity as well. A higher sensitivity of turnover to individual performance for better-governed banks also serves as a check that our governance variable is an appropriate measure of bank governance. We discuss this issue further in the next section.

VI. Robustness Tests and Analysis

a) Alternative Measures of Performance

While management performance can be measured by numerous metrics, the most common accounting measure of performance is return on assets. This paper presents results using both ROA and the four-quarter change in ROA. In additional tests, we replace ROA with return on equity (ROE) and re-estimate our first- and second-stage analyses. Similarly, we run tests replacing change in ROA with change in ROE. In all cases, the results are qualitatively similar.

b) Governance Measure Robustness

The impact of governance on exogenous performance-turnover sensitivity is a key aspect of this paper, so it is important to explore the adequacy of our main governance variable: MRATING. While the variable MRATING is well suited, based on its definition and past evidence associating it with bank governance, it is not a traditional measure in the corporate governance literature, so we perform additional analysis to examine its efficacy as a governance measure.

The results in table 4 show that both the individual and exogenous components of performance are more strongly related to top management turnover for better-governed banks. Because past governance literature has shown stronger performance-turnover sensitivity for better-governed banks, the finding that individual performance is more strongly related to turnover for banks with MRATING values of 1 or 2 suggests that MRATING is a good indicator of bank governance.

In addition, good governance is usually associated with stronger performance, and previous studies (Bhagat and Bolton 2008; Gompers, Ishii, and Metrick 2003) have found positive associations between governance and performance. To the extent that MRATING is a good measure of governance, higher values of MRATING should be associated with worse performance. A correlation analysis (not reported) indicates that MRATING has a negative correlation with ROA and with CH_ROA. This is also consistent with MRATING being a good indicator of bank governance.

c) Governance and Performance-Turnover Sensitivity: Alternative Explanations

Our analysis is consistent with the explanation that better-governed banks are more likely than poorly governed banks to dismiss management in cases of weak exogenously determined performance. But because a weak MRATING may indicate other information about a bank besides its governance, we explore the possibility of other explanations for our results.

One possibility is that because banks with weak MRATING values are likely to have worse performance, performance varies less for these banks. If this is true, it is possible that the finding of less turnover-performance sensitivity for poorly governed banks may be driven simply by the inability of performance to deteriorate further. To explore this issue, we examine the distribution of ROA and CH_ROA for banks with weak and strong values of MRATING. The results indicate that significant variation exists in each of the subsamples and that the variation is greater in banks with weak MRATING values. Therefore, it is not likely that the results are driven by low performance variation in poorly rated (governed) banks.

A second possibility is that MRATING is associated with greater regulatory pressure on bank boards and this pressure drives turnover. While regulatory pressure might be a factor in top management turnover, because such pressure originates from weak governance, the distinction is not critical to our analysis. In addition, such direct pressure, if it exists, is already captured by including MRATING directly in each regression reported in tables 3 and 4. The issue of whether poor governance (as indicated by weak MRATING) leads to enhanced regulatory pressure is not central, because as long as MRATING indicates weak governance, our results still suggest that better-governed banks have stronger exogenous performance-turnover sensitivity.

d) Alternative Peer Group Definitions

We define peer groups by size because it is a simple and straightforward measure that is often used to evaluate relative performance. More refined measures, in addition to introducing noise, may not be practical to implement. Moreover, our first-stage results suggest a clear and systematic variation by size of the impact of explicit and implicit exogenous factors.

Nevertheless, we concede that defining peer groups by size quartiles, while well motivated with Albuquerque (2009), is arbitrary. We also estimate our first- and second-stage results defining peers by size tertiles and size quintiles. The results are very similar.

VII. Conclusions

Our evidence rejects the hypothesis that management performance is judged solely in relative terms for our sample of community banks. These results align with similar evidence in previous studies of large, publicly traded firms. Our results suggest that previous empirical findings have not been driven purely by measurement error and are not relevant only to public firms. Controlling for governance, competition, and outside opportunities does not diminish our results. In fact, better-governed banks are even more likely to dismiss top management during adverse economic conditions. This evidence supports the hypothesis that bad times are more informative of management quality than good times and thus implies that top management dismissals during adverse economic times may not be the result of bad luck. We also show that this evidence is not necessarily inconsistent with the original theory of Holmstrom if one does not impose the restriction that management's value-added should be independent of the exogenous environment. Top managers play a strategic role in the firm, and part of their responsibility is to anticipate and prepare for downturns. It may not be realistic to think that their evaluation should be independent of the exogenous conditions as expected under strict RPE, especially in homogeneous and cyclical industries like banking. The findings in this paper reveal that the theoretical foundation of executive evaluation (compensation and turnover) needs to clearly account for the unique role executives play in the firm.

VIII. References

Albuquerque, A. 2009. Peer Firms in Relative Performance Evaluation. *Journal of Accounting and Economics*, 48(1), 69–89.

Aggarwal, R., and A. Samwick. 1999. Executive Compensation, Strategic Competition, and Relative Performance Evaluation. *Journal of Finance,* 54(6), 1999–2043.

Barro, J., and R. Barro. 1990. Pay, Performance, and Turnover of Bank CEOs. *Journal of Labor Economics,* 8(4), 448–481.

Bhagat, S., and B. Bolton. 2008. Corporate Governance and Firm Performance. *Journal of Corporate Finance*, 14(3), 257–273.

Blackwell, D., J. Brickley, and M. Weisbach. 1994. Accounting Information and Internal Performance Evaluation: Evidence from Texas Banks. *Journal of Accounting and Economics*, 17(3), 331–358.

Bertrand, M., and S. Mullainathan. 2001. Are CEOs Rewarded for Luck? The Ones Without Principals Are. *The Quarterly Journal of Economics*, 116(3), 901–932.

Borokhovich, K., R. Parrino, and T. Trapani. 1996. Outside Directors and CEO Selection. *Journal of Financial and Quantitative Analysis*, 31(3), 337–355.

Cook, D., A. Hogan, and R. Kieschnick. 2004. A Study of the Corporate Governance of Thrifts. *Journal of Banking and Finance*, 28(6), 1247–1271.

Cooper, E. 2008. Monitoring and Governance of Private Banks. *The Quarterly Review of Economics and Finance*, 49(2), 253–264.

Dahya, J., J. McConnell, and N. Travlos. 2002. The Cadbury Committee, Corporate Performance and Top Management Turnover. *Journal of Finance*, 57(1), 461–483.

DeFond, M., and C. Park. 1999. The Effect of Competition on CEO Turnover. *Journal of Accounting and Economics*, 27(1), 35–56.

Ertugrul, M., and K. Krishnan. 2008. *Can CEO Dismissals Be Proactive?* Working paper, available at SSRN: http://ssrn.com/abstract=982005.

Fisman, R., R. Khurana, and M. Rhodes-Kropf. 2005. *Governance and CEO Turnover: Do Something or Do the Right Thing?* Working paper, available at SSRN: http://ssrn.com/abstract=656085 or doi:10.2139/ssrn.656085.

Garvey, G., and T. Milbourn. 2006. Asymmetric Benchmarking in Compensation: Executives Are Rewarded for Good Luck But Not Penalized for Bad. *Journal of Financial Economics*, 82(1), 197–225.

Gibbons, R., and K. Murphy. 1990. Relative Performance Evaluation for Chief Executive Officers. *Industrial and Labor Relations Review*, 43(3), 30S–51S.

Gompers, P., J. Ishii, and A. Metrick. 2003. Corporate Governance and Equity Prices. *Quarterly Journal of Economics,* 118(1), 107–155.

Gunther, J., and R. Moore. 2003. Loss Underreporting and the Auditing Role of Bank Exams. *Journal of Financial Intermediation*, 12(2), 153–177.

Holmstrom, B. 1979. Moral Hazard and Observability. *The Bell Journal of Econometrics*, 10(1), 74–91.

Holmstrom, B. 1982. Moral Hazard in Teams. *The Bell Journal of Econometrics*, 13(2), 324–340.

Houston, J., and C. James. 1993. Management and Organizational Changes in Banking: A Comparison of Regulatory Intervention with Private Creditor Actions in Nonbank Firms. *Carnegie-Rochester Conference Series on Public Policy*, 38(1), 143–178.

Janakiraman, S., R. Lambert, and D. Larcker. 1992. An Empirical Investigation of the Relative Performance Evaluation Hypothesis. *Journal of Accounting Research*, 30(1), 53–69.

Jenter, D., and F. Kanaan. 2008. *CEO Turnover and Relative Performance Evaluation*. NBER working paper no. 12068. Cambridge, MA: National Bureau of Economic Research.

Kaplan, S., and B. Minton. 2006. *How Has CEO Turnover Changed?* NBER working paper no. 12465. Cambridge, MA: National Bureau of Economic Research.

Parrino, R. 1997. CEO Turnover and Outside Succession: A Cross-Sectional Analysis. *Journal of Financial Economics*, 46(2), 165–197.

Prowse, S. 1995. Alternative Methods of Corporate Control in Commercial Banks. *Economic and Financial Policy Review,* QIII, 24–36. Federal Reserve Bank of Dallas.

Weisbach, M. 1988. Outside Directors and CEO Turnover. *Journal of Financial Economics*, 20(1–2), 431–460.

Yatchew, A., and Z. Griliches. 1985. Specification Error in Probit Models. *The Review of Economics and Statistics*, 67(1), 134–139.

Figure 1. Executive Turnover, Average Bank Performance, and Exogenous Factors Across Time

The following figures examine time-series trends in executive turnover, industry performance, and key exogenous factors (unemployment, interest rates, and competition). Data points are based on yearly data for all banks in the sample. Annual return on assets (ROA) is taken from the call reports. Unemployment and interest rate statistics are from the Bureau of Labor Statistics and the Federal Reserve, respectively.

Panel A. Cyclicality of Bank Executive Turnover and Performance

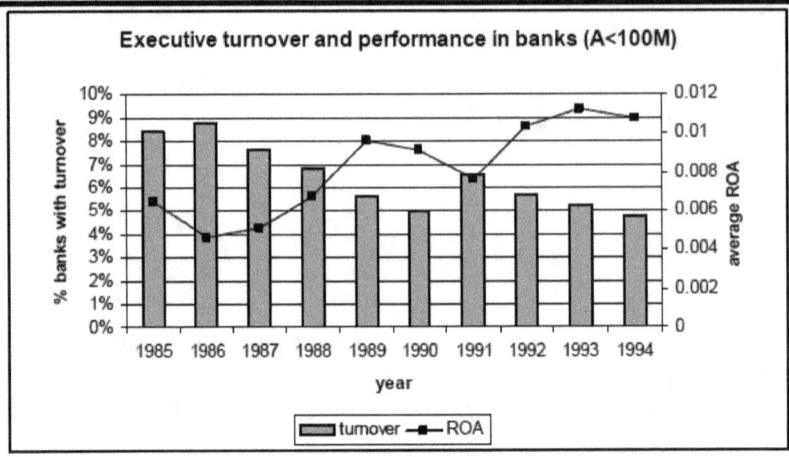

Panel B. Macroeconomic Environment Changes

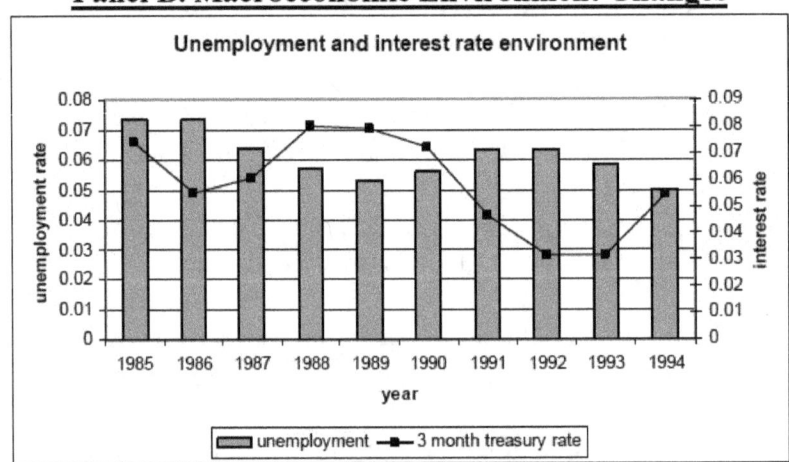

Panel C. Changes in Banks' Competitive Environment

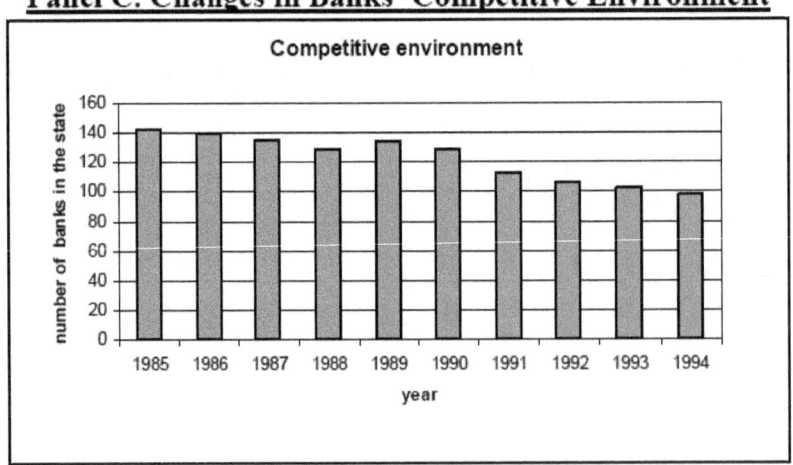

Table 1. Summary Statistics

Statistics in this table are based on call report data from 1985 to 1994 for banks with at most $100 million in assets. Bank performance, macroeconomic, and market variables used in the first stage of the analysis are shown in Panel A for all banks in the sample. The key variables used in the analysis of top management turnover are reported for national banks only, because our measure of governance is based in part on private regulatory variables available only for national banks. The national bank sample is shown in Panel B.

Panel A. Full Sample

Variable	Definition	N	mean	p5	p50	p95
LGASSET	Log Assets	86486	10.38	9.10	10.44	11.44
ROA	Return on Assets	86486	0.78%	-1.22%	0.99%	1.86%
CH_ROA	Return on Assets - 4 Qtr Change	86486	0.03%	-1.24%	0.02%	1.43%
URATE	State Unemployment Rate	86486	6.24%	3.77%	6.17%	9.23%
CH_URATE	State Unemployment Rate - 4 Qtr Change	86486	-0.21%	-1.40%	-0.33%	1.33%
TBILL	3-Month Treasury Bill Rate	86486	5.86%	3.13%	6.07%	7.99%
CH_TBILL	3-Month Treasury Bill Rate - 4 Qtr Change	86486	-0.44%	-2.54%	-0.69%	2.30%
BANKSPCAP	Banks Per 1 Million Persons (by State)	86486	124.78	28.55	121.28	263.20
CH_BANKSPCAP	Banks Per 1 Million Persons (by State) - 4 Qtr Change	86486	-4.89	-13.94	-3.82	0.40

Panel B. National Banks

	Definition	N	mean	p5	p50	p95
EXTURN	Turnover for Any of Top 3 Executives	18944	25.86%	0.00%	0.00%	100.00%
LGASSET	Log Assets	18944	10.58	9.38	10.66	11.50
CH_LGASSET	Log Assets - 4 Qtr Change	18944	0.06	-0.09	0.04	0.26
MRATING	Regulatory Management Rating (1 (best) to 5 (worst))	18944	2.24	1.00	2.00	4.00
CRATIO	Capital Ratio	18944	8.98%	5.15%	8.46%	14.51%
ACQUIRE	Acquired Another Bank in Last Year	18944	2.05%	0.00%	0.00%	0.00%
OWNCHANGE	Change of Ownership of Bank	18944	5.67%	0.00%	0.00%	100.00%
DENOVO	Chartered within Past 5 Years	18944	8.13%	0.00%	0.00%	100.00%
MBHC	Subsidiary of Multi-Bank Holding Company	18944	26.00%	0.00%	0.00%	100.00%
BANKSPCAP	Banks Per 1 Million Persons (by State)	18944	118.86	26.21	113.99	259.41
EXTURNCITY	Turnover for other banks in the city	18944	19.14%	0.00%	0.00%	100.00%

Table 2. Peer Summary Statistics and Univariate Correlations

The table summarizes the variables used in the first-stage regressions and univariate correlations of these variables with our measures of performance. Panel A shows the differences across the four peer groups defined by size quartile. Panel B shows the univariate correlations of our primary performance variable, return on assets (ROA), with the exogenous variables used in the first-stage regression. Panel C shows these same correlations with our secondary performance variable, change in return on assets (CH_ROA). URATE indicates the state unemployment rate. BANKPCAP represents the number of banks per million persons for a given state. TBILL and CH_TBILL denote the 3-month Treasury bill rate and the four-quarter change in this rate. The prefix "PEER" at the beginning of a variable name indicates the average for the peer (i.e., size group); the prefix "YEAR" denotes the industry average for the year. The first-stage regression also includes exogenous variables that do not change by peer group, such as industry average ROA and CH_ROA, TBILL, and CH_TBILL, which we do not report in Panel A.

Panel A. Means by Peer Group

	Size 1 (Smallest)	Size 2	Size 3	Size4 (Largest)
	(N=21,620)	(N=21,625)	(N=21,615)	(N=21,626)
PEER - ROA	0.55%	0.74%	0.85%	0.96%
PEER - CH_ROA	0.06%	0.05%	0.03%	0.00%
URATE	5.87%	6.25%	6.37%	6.48%
CH_URATE	-0.19%	-0.21%	-0.21%	-0.22%
BANKSPCAP	151.99	127.51	116.98	102.64
CH_BANKSPCAP	-5.93	-4.97	-4.64	-4.02

Panel B. Exogenous Factors Univariate Correlation with ROA by Peer Group

	Size 1 (Smallest)	Size 2	Size 3	Size4 (Largest)
PEER_ROA	24.17%	23.24%	20.15%	18.64%
CH_PEER_ROA	13.59%	8.36%	5.33%	0.25%
YEAR_ROA	22.94%	22.29%	19.57%	18.25%
CH_YEAR_ROA	9.91%	8.91%	7.49%	7.56%
URATE	-16.85%	-17.16%	-16.18%	-13.72%
CH_URATE	-6.23%	-5.19%	-7.57%	-8.30%
TBILL	-9.44%	-11.05%	-8.33%	-8.93%
CH_TBILL	5.02%	3.82%	5.28%	5.22%
BANKSPCAP	1.71%	1.23%	-0.74%	-5.73%
CH_BANKSPCAP	-0.68%	0.16%	3.56%	2.70%

Panel C. Exogenous Factors Univariate Correlation with CH_ROA by Peer Group

	Size 1 (Smallest)	Size 2	Size 3	Size4 (Largest)
PEER_ROA	4.25%	5.27%	6.49%	8.82%
CH_PEER_ROA	9.48%	12.39%	12.51%	11.31%
YEAR_ROA	4.43%	5.76%	7.50%	9.18%
CH_YEAR_ROA	9.76%	10.57%	11.17%	11.68%
URATE	-1.61%	-3.78%	-5.62%	-6.43%
CH_URATE	-3.21%	-2.31%	-6.05%	-7.98%
TBILL	-1.92%	-5.19%	-4.77%	-6.22%
CH_TBILL	4.31%	0.81%	2.07%	2.09%
BANKSPCAP	-4.60%	-6.65%	-3.18%	-5.35%
CH_BANKSPCAP	-1.04%	-0.20%	-1.11%	-2.38%

Table 3. Multivariate Tests: Turnover and Performance

Each column in this table shows logistic regression results of executive turnover during the year (EXTURN) on performance and controls. Performance is measured by EX_PERF and IND_PERF, which represent the exogenous and individual components of performance as decomposed by equation (6). Columns 1–3 show results using return on assets (ROA) as the measure of performance; columns 4–6 show results using the four-quarter difference in return on assets (CHROA) as the measure of performance. The variable MRATING is a measure of bank governance (higher values indicate worse governance). LGASSET and CH_LGASSET represent log of assets and the four-quarter change in log assets. CRATIO indicates the capital ratio. ACQUIRE, OWNCHANGE, and DENOVO control for whether a bank recently acquired another bank, whether the bank ownership recently changed, and whether the bank was recently chartered, respectively. MBHC indicates affiliation with a multibank holding company, and BANKSPCAP indicates the number of banks per million persons in the state. EXTURNCITY indicates the percentage of other banks in the city with turnover during the year. T-stats are presented in parentheses below each regression coefficient. The asterisks indicate significance of the regression coefficients. Significance at the 1 percent level is indicated by ***; ** and * indicate significance at the 5 percent and 10 percent levels, respectively. All results are reported with robust standard errors.

Performance Measure	(1) ROA	(2) ROA	(3) ROA	(4) CHROA	(5) CHROA	(6) CHROA
IND_PERF	-30.27 ***	-23.76 ***	-23.64 ***	-13.36 ***	-12.26 ***	-12.25 ***
	-(16.32)	-(12.42)	-(12.34)	-(7.40)	-(7.21)	-(7.21)
EX_PERF	-43.59 ***	-39.33 ***	-38.60 ***	-68.92 ***	-70.47 ***	-68.24 ***
	-(6.53)	-(5.86)	-(5.72)	-(5.69)	-(5.79)	-(5.49)
MRATING		0.28 ***	0.28 ***		0.38 ***	0.38 ***
		(10.55)	(10.58)		(15.47)	(15.47)
LGASSET	-0.09 **	-0.04	-0.11	-0.27 ***	-0.18 ***	-0.23 ***
	-(2.54)	-(1.17)	-(1.27)	-(9.64)	-(6.37)	-(2.96)
CHLGASSET	-0.65 ***	-0.49 ***	-0.55 ***	-0.81 ***	-0.50 ***	-0.55 ***
	-(4.09)	-(3.12)	-(3.21)	-(4.79)	-(3.08)	-(3.08)
CRATIO	-3.23 ***	-1.99 ***	-2.03 ***	-6.94 ***	-4.15 ***	-4.18 ***
	-(4.92)	-(3.06)	-(3.12)	-(10.32)	-(6.32)	-(6.37)
ACQUIRE	0.29 **	0.28 **	0.28 **	0.35 ***	0.31 **	0.31 **
	(2.32)	(2.22)	(2.22)	(2.77)	(2.45)	(2.43)
OWNCHANGE	0.43 ***	0.44 ***	0.44 ***	0.42 ***	0.43 ***	0.43 ***
	(6.20)	(6.25)	(6.24)	(6.06)	(6.14)	(6.14)
DENOVO	0.31 ***	0.39 ***	0.39 ***	0.72 ***	0.72 ***	0.72 ***
	(4.72)	(5.82)	(5.84)	(11.73)	(11.62)	(11.61)
MBHC	0.31 ***	0.39 ***	0.39 ***	0.28 ***	0.40 ***	0.39 ***
	(7.95)	(9.75)	(9.69)	(7.15)	(9.91)	(9.84)
BANKSPCAP	0.00 ***	0.00 **	0.00 **	0.00 ***	0.00 ***	0.00 ***
	-(2.97)	-(2.41)	-(2.47)	-(4.76)	-(4.08)	-(4.07)
EXTURNCITY	1.04 ***	1.03 ***	1.03 ***	1.09 ***	1.07 ***	1.06 ***
	(18.63)	(18.48)	(18.44)	(19.64)	(19.07)	(19.05)
Constant Term	0.19	-1.12 ***	-0.36	2.16 ***	0.03	0.77
	(0.55)	-(3.02)	-(0.39)	(6.83)	(0.09)	(0.86)
Peer Fixed Effects	NO	NO	YES	NO	NO	YES
Observations	18942	18942	18942	18942	18942	18942
Pseudo R-Square	6.19%	6.73%	6.74%	5.09%	6.26%	6.27%
Chi-Square Statistic	1171.26	1295.97	1295.97	1026.19	1243.92	1244.40

Table 4. Multivariate Tests: Turnover, Performance, and Governance

This table shows logistic regression results for executive turnover during the year (EXTURN) regressed on individual performance (IND_PERF), exogenous performance (EX_PERF), and controls. The results are similar to those in table 3, except that each component of performance is interacted with dummies based on our measure of governance (MRATING). A good MRATING is 1 or 2, while a poor MRATING is 3, 4, or 5. Performance is measured as return on assets (ROA) and change in return on assets (CH_ROA) in columns 1–3 and columns 4–6, respectively. LGASSET and CH_LGASSET represent log of assets and the four-quarter change in log assets. CRATIO indicates the capital ratio. ACQUIRE, OWNCHANGE, DENOVO, and MBHC control for whether a bank recently acquired another bank, whether the bank ownership recently changed, whether the bank is affiliated with a multibank holding company, and whether the bank was recently chartered, respectively. BANKSPCAP and EXTURNCITY indicate the number of banks per million persons in the state and the percentage of other banks in the city with turnover during the year. The asterisks indicate significance of the regression coefficients. Significance at the 1 percent level is indicated by ***; ** and * indicate significance at the 5 percent and 10 percent levels, respectively. Coefficients are reported with robust standard errors.

Performance Measure	(1) ROA	(2) ROA	(3) ROA	(4) CHROA	(5) CHROA	(6) CHROA
IND_PERF x Good MRATING	-34.17 ***	-32.32 ***	-32.22 ***	-17.15 ***	-16.85 ***	-16.86 ***
	-(11.14)	-(10.59)	-(10.55)	-(5 98)	-(5.67)	-(5.68)
IND_PERF x Poor MRATING	-22.47 ***	-18.82 ***	-18.68 ***	-11.87 ***	-10.22 ***	-10.18 ***
	-(10.18)	-(8.37)	-(8.29)	-(5.13)	-(4.98)	-(4.97)
EX_PERF x Good MRATING	-58.90 ***	-46.30 ***	-45.57 ***	-98.13 ***	-90.64 ***	-88.11 ***
	-(8.49)	-(6.42)	-(6.29)	-(7.03)	-(6.16)	-(5.91)
EX_PERF x Poor MRATING	-10.85	-32.75 ***	-31.86 ***	-11.66	-38.48 **	-36.62 *
	-(1.42)	-(3.93)	-(3.82)	-(0.55)	-(2.00)	-(1.88)
MRATING		0.24 ***	0.24 ***		0.38 ***	0.38 ***
		(6.25)	(6.26)		(15.29)	(15.30)
LGASSET	-0.06 *	-0.04	-0.11	-0.27 ***	-0.18 ***	-0.23 ***
	-(1.79)	-(1.15)	-(1.33)	-(9.46)	-(6.30)	-(2.99)
CH_LGASSET	-0.61 ***	-0.54 ***	-0.60 ***	-0.81 ***	-0.50 ***	-0.55 ***
	-(3.80)	-(3.39)	-(3.48)	-(4.80)	-(3.08)	-(3.10)
CAPRAT	-2.65 ***	-2.01 ***	-2.06 ***	-6.86 ***	-4.13 ***	-4.16 ***
	-(4.06)	-(3.08)	-(3.15)	-(10.23)	-(6.29)	-(6.34)
ACQUIRE	0.31 **	0.29 **	0.29 **	0.35 ***	0.31 **	0 31 **
	(2.43)	(2.31)	(2.30)	(2.84)	(2.49)	(2.47)
OWNCHANGE	0.43 ***	0.44 ***	0.44 ***	0.42 ***	0.43 ***	0.43 ***
	(6.15)	(6.23)	(6.21)	(6.00)	(6.10)	(6.09)
DENOVO	0.32 ***	0.35 ***	0.35 ***	0.74 ***	0.74 ***	0.74 ***
	(4.79)	(5.23)	(5.24)	(11.90)	(11.82)	(11.81)
MBHC	0.36 ***	0.39 ***	0.39 ***	0.28 ***	0.40 ***	0.39 ***
	(9.05)	(9.68)	(9.62)	(7.15)	(9.88)	(9.82)
BANKSPCAP	0.00 ***	0.00 **	0.00 ***	0.00 ***	0.00 ***	0.00 ***
	-(2.81)	-(2.50)	-(2.57)	-(4.54)	-(3.94)	-(3.93)
EXTURNCITY	1.03 ***	1.03 ***	1.03 ***	1.08 ***	1.06 ***	1.06 ***
	(18.45)	(18.38)	(18.34)	(19.58)	(19.04)	(19.01)
Constant Term	-0.12	-0.99 ***	-0.17	2.13 ***	0.01	0.79
	-(0.33)	-(2.61)	-(0.18)	(6.71)	(0.04)	(0.88)
Peer Fixed Effects	NO	NO	YES	NO	NO	YES
Observations	18942	18942	18942	18942	18942	18942
Pseudo R-Square	6.62%	6.82%	6.82%	5.16%	6.30%	6.31%
Chi-Square Statistic	1267.43	1312.93	1313.20	1037.60	1249.77	1250.42